COLONIAL PEOPLE

The Colonial Woodworker

LAURA L. SULLIVAN

Cavendish
Square

New York

Published in 2016 by Cavendish Square Publishing, LLC
243 5th Avenue, Suite 136, New York, NY 10016

First Edition

Website: cavendishsq.com

This publication represents the opinions and views of the author based on his or her personal experience, knowledge, and research. The information in this book serves as a general guide only. The author and publisher have used their best efforts in preparing this book and disclaim liability rising directly or indirectly from the use and application of this book.

CPSIA Compliance Information: Batch #WS15CSQ

All websites were available and accurate when this book was sent to press.

Library of Congress Cataloging-in-Publication Data

Sullivan, Laura L., 1974-
The colonial woodworker / Laura L. Sullivan.
pages cm. — (Colonial people)
Includes bibliographical references and index.
ISBN 978-1-50260-484-2 (hardcover) ISBN 978-1-50260-485-9 (ebook)
1. Woodworkers—United States—History—Juvenile literature. 2. Woodwork—United States—History—Juvenile literature.
3. United States—Social life and customs—To 1775—Juvenile literature.
4. United States—History—Colonial period, ca. 1600-1775—Juvenile literature. I. Title.
TT180.S85 2016
684'.080973—dc23
2014047265

Editorial Director: David McNamara
Editor: Andrew Coddington
Copy Editor: Cynthia Roby
Art Director: Jeffrey Talbot
Designer: Stephanie Flecha
Senior Production Manager: Jennifer Ryder-Talbot
Production Editor: Renni Johnson
Photo Research: J8 Media

The photographs in this book are used by permission and through the courtesy of: Universal History Archive/UIG/Getty Images, cover; North Wind Picture Archives, 4; Ann Ronan Pictures/Hulton Archive/Getty Images, 7; Hulton Achive/Getty Images, 8; North Wind Picture Archives, 9; MPI/ Archive Photos/Getty Images, 11; Fototeca Gilardi/Stockbyte/Getty Images, 14; Colonial Williamsburg Foundation, 15, 19, 21; Jebulon/File:Fauteuil Jacob cabinet méridienne Versailles.jpg/Wikimedia Commons, 23; Andy Roland/iStock/Thinkstock, 26; Ronstik/iStock/Thinkstock, 28; Colonial Williamsburg Foundation, 32, 33; Hulton Archive/Getty Images, 36; Cate Gillon/Getty Images, 38; Colonial Williamsburg Foundation, 40.

Printed in the United States of America

CONTENTS

ONE

Land of Trees, Land of Opportunity

There is a story that is often told about what many Native American tribes thought was the real reason the British **colonists** came to America. They believed that the settlers had cut down every last one of the trees in their home country, and had journeyed to the New World to find a place full of trees. They weren't completely wrong.

After the **Ice Age**, England was dominated by forests. It is estimated that woodland made up of hazel, birch, and oak trees covered about seventy-five percent of the land. Not long after, humans began to heavily colonize England. After that, burning and clearing for agriculture quickly reduced the number of trees. Over the centuries, England became more and more devoted to farmland and pastureland. By the start of the Iron Age, around 1200 BCE,

The abundance of trees—and thus the promise of wood—was one of the attractions of the New World.

forests only covered about fifty percent of England. By around 1086 CE, only fifteen percent of England was forested. Even yew wood for the famous English longbows had to be imported from Spain. Trees—an extremely valuable resource—had become a scarce commodity. As often happens, they were seized by the wealthy.

Trees for Noblemen and Ships

In the early seventeenth century, when large numbers of British colonists began to settle in North America, forests in England were largely in the hands of noblemen. Forested land was on the private estates of dukes, earls, and lords. Trees were considered money in the bank. They were carefully tended and when the nobleman needed money he would order a certain amount of **timber** to be cut. New trees would be planted in place of the felled trees, but would take dozens of years to reach maturity.

Wood from England's precious trees was used to create a range of items from houses and **utilitarian** products to precious works of art that included fine cabinets, clocks, and musical instruments. But one of the most important uses of wood in England was for shipbuilding. The mighty English oak, with its hard wood that resisted rot, helped make England into a great global power. The country's merchant fleet—which brought England vast fortunes—and

The few remaining tracts of forested land in England were kept for the pleasure and profit of the nobles.

the navy's warships were constructed from oak. Oak trees were so valuable for shipbuilding that the Spanish once hoped to defeat the British by burning down their forests. No oaks trees, no ships. And without ships, the island nation would crumble. The plan failed, and Britain retained her power over the seas.

Better than Gold

Some naive settlers might have hoped to discover gold when they landed in North America. The more practical colonists were lured by the abundance of natural resources, particularly trees. Treatises and advertisements promoting America to potential colonists expressed the abundance of tall, strong oaks, as well as beech, elm, and walnut; more exotic woods such as sassafras, and many trees they couldn't identify. It was clear that the North American colonies would be a **woodworker's** paradise.

In the early years of settlement, trees provided two basic needs: shelter and fuel. Trees were felled to make log homes, and later more sophisticated and finely made plank dwellings. Wood was also the primary fuel, and provided heat in the brutal New England winters and cooking fires year round. Wood was also

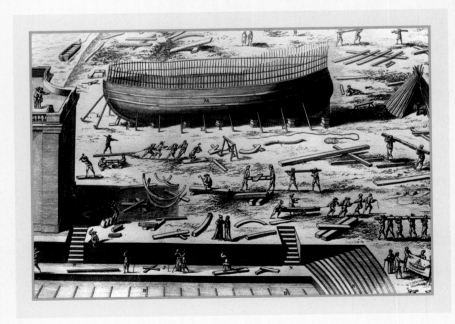

Britain, which was said to "rule the waves," depended on its scarce supply of timber to build its mighty ships.

Almost all early settlers were amateur woodworkers, making their own log cabins.

necessary for other colonial industries. Burning wood or charcoal (made by slowly heating wood without letting it actually burn) was used to bake bricks and to fire ceramics.

Later, when the colonies were more established and residents moved from mere survival to creating a society that rivaled the major cities of Europe, craftsmen and artisans began to come into their own. Woodworkers of all kinds flourished. Houses became works of art, boasting fine wooden staircases and clever cupboards. Furniture making became a flourishing trade, and the colonies developed their own distinct styles. The majority of goods in a colonist's world were made of wood, and the people who made those items were valued.

The Benefits and Limitations of Wood

Though the focus of this book is on the more useful side of woodworking—the creation of furniture, tools, barrels, and more—there is also a long history of woodworking as a fine art. For delicate artistic carvings, cunning cabinets, and rougher everyday wood creations, a craftsman had to understand the qualities and characteristics of the wood with which he was working. Any kind of wood can be carved, but each has its own peculiarities. Softwoods such as pine are easy to shape, but not as durable. Hardwoods such as oak are harder to carve, but less likely to break.

Woodworkers also have to pay attention to the grain of the wood, or the growth rings that determine in which direction the wood is strongest. Delicate details of a wooden sculpture should follow the grain for added strength. So should any load-bearing pieces of wood.

A Carpenter.

Wooden objects are less likely to survive through generations than those made of metal or stone. Wood is subject to rot from water damage, insects, or dry rot, and is usually destroyed in fires. Still, it is a versatile material that was widely available and generally inexpensive. So in the colonies as well as in Europe, wood was a common choice for the construction of a wide variety of goods.

Colonial woodworkers had to carefully consider the direction of the grain, as well as other characteristics of the wood, when shaping it into artistic or useful items.

A Variety of Trades

There were many aspects to woodworking. On the grandest scale, special woodworkers called shipwrights made everything from rowboats to mighty merchant ships. Carpenters constructed houses. Some woodworkers specialized in the delicate art of bending wood. These craftsmen included wheelwrights who made wheels for wagons and carriages, as well as coopers, who made the barrels that virtually everything was stored in at the time. Woodworkers partnered with blacksmiths to make tools such as axes and hammers. They turned their attention to finer crafts, partnering with clockmakers to combine intricate machinery with a beautiful wooden facade. They even made musical instruments like harpsichords and spinets.

The colonies attracted many skilled woodworkers, mostly from Britain but also from elsewhere in Europe. They trained the new generations of woodworkers. By the time the colonies gained their independence, there was a thriving community of many types of woodworkers in most of the major cities.

TWO

Becoming a Woodworker

Today, few things are made by hand. Most household objects and items that people use every day are made in factories by machines. Often they are made out of plastic, a material whose shape, flexibility, and texture can be altered to fit almost any use from dishes to tools to furniture. Other materials such as metal can also be easily shaped in the modern era to fit many needs. However, in colonial America, both the materials and techniques were much more limited. A young person who wanted to have a career molding materials into useful shapes had a few basic options. He could be a blacksmith, or a person who works with hot metals such as iron or steel in a forge. A blacksmith might make nails and horseshoes. Or he could be a tinsmith, pewtersmith, or silversmith, working with those metals to create objects of utility or beauty.

Woodworking was a desirable skill in colonial America. Many young men were apprenticed to the craft.

One of the most common crafting professions was that of woodworker. It could be a very profitable career path for a young person. Woodworking became a more popular career choice in the colonies than it had been in Britain, because there was a much greater supply of wood freely available. Also, many people became woodworkers or carpenters out of necessity. When they arrived in the New World, they had to make almost everything from scratch. They had to learn to chop down trees, shape boards, make furniture—

all the things they needed for their new life. As the colonies became more settled and towns prospered, people began to specialize more. Fine woodworkers who could create expertly crafted furniture, stairways, or mantles were in high demand. Woodworkers were also needed for other specialties. They learned to be coopers, cart and carriage makers, wheelwrights, and instrument makers.

The Apprentice Woodworker

There were several ways in which a young person could become a professional woodworker in Colonial America. During the colonial period (roughly from the founding of Jamestown in 1607 to the beginning of the American Revolutionary War in 1775) the **guild** system was in effect in Britain and much of Europe. The colonies, however, did not have an official system and set of laws or standards governing the trades. Roughly, though, they followed the traditional system of apprenticeship.

An **apprentice** is a person who is legally bound to a **master** craftsman for a fixed period, in order to learn that craft. A young

A young apprentice would be bound to a master woodworker for about seven years.

man in colonial America might show an aptitude for working with wood. Or, his parents might simply decide that was a good career choice for him. Parents usually paid the master a sum of money to take on their child.

Poor children, orphans, and those who were under the jurisdiction of the court were also usually apprenticed. The Virginia Poor Law of 1672 stated that the courts could bind as apprentices any child whose parents could not afford to raise them. In 1705, the Orphan Act allowed the court to apprentice any orphans who did not inherit enough money to support themselves. The parish, or village, then usually paid the master a fee to take the orphan child.

Apprentice Rules

A young woodworker would be apprenticed for anywhere between five and nine years. The average was seven. Traditionally, he would be bound at age fourteen, so that he could train for seven years and emerge at the "legal age of majority," which was twenty-one, a skilled craftsman. Shorter apprenticeships were common in the colonies. Orphans, though, might have a long apprenticeship, as they tended to be apprenticed very young.

The young apprentice woodworker was bound by many rules. He had to agree to work for the master woodworker without any pay for the term of his apprenticeship. He was not free to leave the workshop without his master's permission. He had to obey his master in all things. His role and treatment were somewhere between a member of the family and a servant. He might eat and live with the family, or he might have to live and eat in the shop. Some even continued to live at home, and were day-apprentices. Masters were free to beat their apprentices but were also responsible for keeping them decently fed and clothed. Just as with any family or business, people were treated in a variety of ways.

From Apprentice to Master

The apprentice woodworker would begin by learning fundamental details. He was schooled about the different types of wood and their qualities. He would also begin to master the basics of woodworking. A young apprentice furniture maker, for example, would learn the two basic skills of **turning** and **joining**. As he gained experience, he would help his master more and more. Eventually, he would be able to equal—or even surpass—his master.

After his apprenticeship had expired, a young woodworker would often be given a suit of clothes, a set of woodworking tools, and maybe a sum of money. He would then be free to work for himself and charge money for the items he created.

In Europe at the time, an apprentice graduated to **journeyman** after finishing his contract. He would then work for several more years, often traveling widely to increase his skill, until he created his **masterpiece**, or supreme achievement, which would qualify him to become a master. In the colonies, however, the process was less formal. A young woodworker would usually work for wages as an employee as soon as he finished his apprenticeship. He was then sometimes considered a journeyman. Or, if he could afford it, he could set up his own shop right away, at which point he would be considered a master woodworker.

Were There Female Woodworkers?

There are two answers to this question. One is: *We don't know.* Records are incomplete. But just because something didn't survive on paper to the modern day does not mean it didn't happen. We do know that most professional woodworkers (and most professionals in any job at the time) were male.

The second answer is: *Probably.* There are certainly records of girls being apprenticed at various trades. Many were in textile trades, such as weaving. Standard apprentice contracts

in the colonies and in Britain had a blank space where the master could insert "he" or "she." A period illustration from Ben Franklin's *Poor Richard's Almanack* on display at the James Geddy House in Colonial Williamsburg shows four blacksmiths working at an anvil, one of who is female.

Most businesses were family affairs, in which everyone took part to some extent. In a woodworker's shop, the women might help with accounts, or they might even learn how to work with wood themselves. A daughter of a woodworker might not be an official apprentice, but if her father needed help in his shop, it is likely that she would learn at least a little about the business. Some might even earn a master's skills without the official title. Frequently, a widow would keep a business going after her husband's death.

During colonial times, though, a woman's primary role was as a wife and mother. Very few women worked outside the home. Most of those who did were likely working from necessity rather than choice.

Above: *there were probably at least a few women employed as woodworkers, such as this cooper in Colonial Williamsburg.*

THREE

A Day in the Life of a Colonial Woodworker

Though there were many specialties of woodworking, the furniture maker typifies the daily life of a colonial woodworker. The term cabinetmaker is often used to refer to a furniture maker, but cabinetmakers specifically created types of furniture that incorporated other parts—that is, pieces that have either drawers, such as desks and secretaries, or doors, such as a wardrobe. Some woodworkers were all-purpose furniture makers, creating chairs, cabinets, and other furniture items. Some were specialists, who might partner with other specialists to create a wide range of furnishings. Two of the basic specialties of woodworking are turning and joining.

A turner creates wooden objects using a **lathe**—a machine that rotates the object being worked on its axis. In most types of woodworking, the piece of wood remains still. In turning, the wood

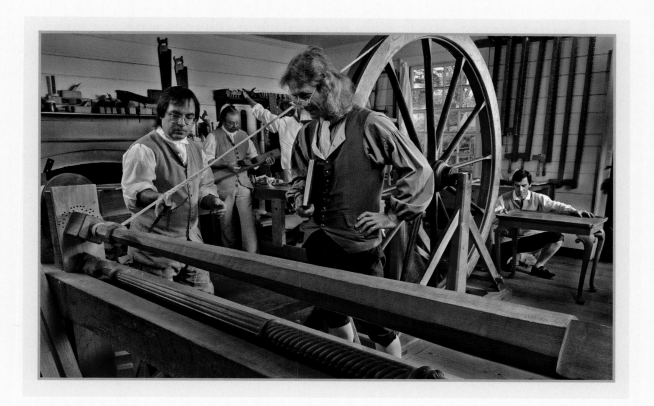

Woodworkers known as turners used a rotating lathe to shape wood.
Here, the master woodworker on the right examines his employee's work.

spins while the woodworker holds a tool to the moving wood to shape it. Early lathes were spun by hand, so the woodworker had to use his feet to hold his tools. A great improvement came with a lathe operated by a foot pedal. This left the craftsman's hands free. Larger lathes were operated by two people—one turning the lathe, the other shaping the wood.

A wood turner could create many intricate shapes with the lathe. Turners could create chair legs and other chair parts, bedposts, candlesticks, spindles for staircases, and many other items. Turners could also hollow out wood to make bowls.

A joiner was the woodworker who specialized in fitting wood together without any metal fasteners. The place where two pieces of wood come together is called the joint. While a carpenter who made a house would use nails for the framework and hinges for doors, a joiner cut wood in such a way that the pieces fit perfectly together. Some joiners use binders or adhesives to make sure the wooden components stay tightly together. Others rely on precise fitting to interlock wooden pieces.

A Fine Finish

A furniture maker had to know about more than manipulating wood. Most furniture had finishes and decorative additions that were done by the woodworker.

At every stage, and at the end of construction, the wood would be sanded and polished to give it a smooth texture and allow the wood grain to show to best effect. Colonial woodworkers used sandpaper and glass paper—which was made of crushed glass adhering to paper. They also used a plant known as a horsetail. The horsetail has a high silica content, which mimics sandpaper, and can be used to give a fine sanding to woods. Horsetails were used by Native Americans to sand and polish their wooden crafts.

When the piece was complete, it was time to apply various finishes, polishes, and decorations. Beeswax was commonly used, because it was readily available. It was sometimes mixed with turpentine to make it easier to work with. The wax might be rubbed in with cork and finely ground brick dust. Most other finishes had to be imported.

Varnish created a protective coating on wood. It usually consisted of a resin (sap or other fluid from pants or trees, usually conifers such as pines), a drying oil such as linseed or walnut oil, and a solvent or thinner such as turpentine.

Some furniture might be gilded, or lightly covered with gold foil, such as this chair from around 1710, which was made in the Rococo style.

A glossy finish could be achieved with **shellac**, which is made from the excretions of the lac bug. Several layers were applied each day, with time to dry in between, until there were up to eighteen coats. This would be sanded and finished with wax. Since the lac insects are found mostly in India and Thailand, shellac had to be imported. It was quite expensive, and only became more common late in the period.

High-end furniture might be **gilded**, or decorated with thin sheets of gold. Rabbit-skin glue (made from boiling connective tissues such as tendons and ligaments) and chalk were mixed together to make a gesso—a primer or base—for the gold leaf. Less expensive furniture might be painted.

Hours of Work

These projects were all very labor intensive. Woodworkers in the Colonial Williamsburg cabinetry and furniture-making shop estimated that a large secretary-type desk would involve about five hundred total hours of work. Three or four people might spend ten to twelve hours a day, for two or three weeks, working on the same piece. A simple chair might take about thirty hours of work, while an ornate chair with intricately turned legs and decorative carvings might take eighty hours.

Master woodworkers owned most furniture-making shops. They might have been formally apprenticed in Europe before coming to North America, or they might have been trained in the colonies. They probably had at least one, if not several assistants. There might be one or two apprentices, as well as a trained journeyman who hadn't saved enough money to start his own shop. Beyond that, master woodworkers' families were likely involved in the business. Their sons were likely trained to follow in their footsteps. If there were no sons (or if they didn't show any talent or interest) then the daughters, if interested, would help out. Girls might learn the trade, but would probably stop working at it once they married—unless they married another woodworker.

The Woodworker's Shop

A typical shop had two rooms. The manual labor would mostly go on in the back—where the furniture was actually made. The front room, a type of showroom, would be to show off their wares and to conduct business. Earlier in the history of the colonies, almost all furniture was **commissioned**. That is, someone, for example, would come into the shop and tell the woodworker that they needed a dining table and set of chairs. The master woodworker would consult with them about exactly what they wanted, possibly take a

Furniture was usually made in a back room, while finished products were on display in a front room.

down payment, and then get to work. The furniture would be built in the exact size, shape, and material that the customer requested.

Later, though, many began to make furniture on **speculation**, meaning to make a piece that wasn't already ordered by a buyer. Particularly in large, wealthy cities such as Boston or Philadelphia, master woodworkers liked to have beautiful furniture on display to tempt shoppers. A rich merchant might not need an inlaid curio cabinet with claw feet, but once he saw it, the woodworker hoped he couldn't resist.

A Woodworker's Tools

A colonial woodworker was very proud of his tools, and made sure they were kept in excellent condition. Many are still in use today.

The *chisel* is a tool with a cutting edge on its tip. It is often driven into the wood with a mallet, or hammer.

A *gouge* is a variation on the chisel that has a curved blade. There are many different gouge shapes and widths, which create different designs in wood.

Awls and *gimlets* were tools for drilling small holes in wood.

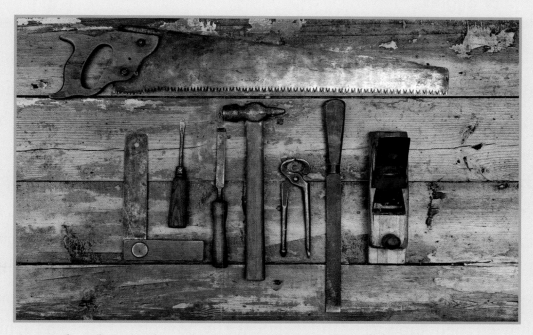

A woodworker used a wide variety of specialized hand tools.

An awl is usually smooth, while a gimlet had a screw at the end. An *augur* is a large version of a gimlet.

A *froe* is an L-shaped tool used to split wood along the grain. It is used to cut wooden shingles and planks.

A *plane* is a wood-shaping tool that can remove very thin shavings from a piece of wood. It can be used to thin the wood, or simply smooth the surface.

Accuracy was important to the woodworker. *Calipers* and *compasses* could be used to measure pieces and keep them uniform. *Bevels* and *squares* were used to check the accuracy of angles.

The early colonies didn't have many (or any) professional furniture makers, cabinetmakers, or fine woodworkers. Most people didn't have the money or the leisure to need anything but the most basic furniture. The more prosperous imported their furniture from Britain. But the number of fine woodworkers increased in the second half of the seventeenth century. Then, by the mid-eighteenth century, only about one-third of furniture was still being imported from Britain. This percentage soon dropped even lower as the colonists began to resent British rule. Revolution was looming, and many colonists showed their support of independence by boycotting British furniture and supporting local woodworkers.

FOUR

The Woodworking Community

Furniture makers were only one part of the woodworking community. Many other professional craftsmen made their living by working with wood, and many more worked with wood on an amateur level, out of necessity. Woodworkers also teamed with other craftsmen such as metalworkers to create finished products.

In the earliest colonial period every settler was, to a greater or lesser degree, a woodworker. The fundamental tool was the ax. Using this simple tool, a colonist could fell trees, then square off the logs into beams that could be used to make log cabins. In the beginning, people built their own homes or banded together with their neighbors to make houses or barns. Later, house building became a specialty, and people hired carpenters to make their homes.

Shipbuilders

Woodworkers branched into many specialties, large and small. Shipbuilders, or shipwrights, took advantage of the abundance of oaks to establish a boat-building industry. This business relied on woodworkers to shape the oaks into planks, use a single mighty trunk to make a mast, and craft and join all of the wooden rigging that helped support the sails.

The ship-building carpenters were part of a community of skilled workers. First, a designer had to use engineering skills to design a seaworthy ship. Then workers known as fasteners drove trunnels (tree nails, or wooden nails) into wooden planks through holes the borers had drilled. Dubbers smoothed the surfaces. Then the caulkers and oakum boys filled in gaps with a mix of hemp fibers and **pitch**. The shipbuilding industry also supported rope makers, sailmakers, and the merchants and fisherman who used the ships.

Wainwrights

Woodworkers also played a valuable part in land-based transportation. In the early colonial period, most travel was done on foot or horseback. The road system wasn't good enough for wheeled vehicles. However, around the time of the American Revolutionary War, roads improved and more and more territory was settled and inhabited. There was a new demand for makers of wagons and carriages.

Carriage making combined several disciplines. Woodworkers made the main body and the wheels. Metal workers made the chains and springs that provided suspension and made a carriage comfortable. Leatherworkers made harnesses for the horses that pulled the coach or wagon. Artists would cover the exterior of a fancy carriage with decorative scenes or gilding. Makers of wagons and carriages were also called wainwrights.

Wheelwrights

Wheels were very difficult to make, as they involved combining bent pieces of wood into a perfect circle using precise geometric measurements. The wheels had to be sturdily made to withstand the rough conditions of even decent roads of the time. The hub, spokes, and the outer portion of the wheel were all made of wood. The wooden wheel was usually bound with iron, so the woodworker and the blacksmith had to work very closely together. An iron hoop was constructed to exactly fit the wooden wheel. The iron hoop was then heated, causing it to expand slightly. It was hammered onto the wheel and then doused with cold water to make the metal quickly shrink and tighten. This process bound the wood and iron firmly

Wheelwrights had to curve wood into precise, very strong circles for wagon and carriage wheels.

together. The iron hoop was called a tire. The word eventually came to be used for rubber wheels for bicycles and automobiles.

Coopers

Another valuable branch of the woodworking family were the coopers, or barrel makers. In addition to barrels, a cooper made casks, butter churns, hogsheads, tubs, and many other similarly shaped items. They were all made with staved wood—pieces of wood that are cut into narrow lengths and joined side by side to form the barrel walls. Heating and binding the staves in just the right way caused them to bow out in the middle into a typical barrel shape. Coopers sometimes worked with hoopers—metalsmiths who fitted the metal rings around the barrels to help bind them. Nearly everything that was stored or transported on a ship used barrels, making this woodworking profession one of the most important in the colonies.

There were several specialties of coopering. The simplest kind was called slack or dry coopering. These woodworkers made barrels for transporting or storing dry goods such as grains, apples, and other foodstuffs. These kept the goods safe from rodents and other

Coopers heated the barrels to achieve a bowed shape in the wood.

pests, but were not airtight. The next level was the dry-tight cooper. He made barrels for dry goods that kept moisture out. This was useful for items such as gunpowder, which would be ruined if it became damp.

More specialized coopers made barrels for wet goods. A white cooper made containers that would hold liquid, such as butter churns and washtubs. However, these could not be used for wet storage. The tight, or wet, cooper made casks such as hogsheads that could transport and store liquids such as wine or cider. They could even handle the increased pressure of fermentation.

Many Woodworking Specialties

Coffin making was another woodworking specialty, though more often in the earlier colonial period coffins were made by the general carpenter. The carpenter sometimes handled the entire funeral, eventually leading to funeral service as its own business.

Woodworkers sometimes turned their skills to other even more specialized trades. Items such as clocks and musical instruments were usually made in Europe and imported by the colonies. As cities grew and colonial markets expanded, specialists came to America. Clockmakers had to pay close attention not only to the technical components inside their clocks, but also to the outside, which was generally made of wood. Sometimes a clockmaker and woodworking specialist worked together.

Gradually, instrument makers began to establish shops in the colonies. The first American violin was made in 1759. Specialized woodworkers made keyboard instruments, such as the harpsichord and spinet, which were popular with the wealthiest colonists.

It Starts with the Woodsmen

Whatever their specialty, woodworkers relied on woodsmen to go out into the wilderness and cut down the trees the skilled artisans needed for their wood. A woodsman generally used a felling ax to cut down a tree. He could make a small cut, called a notch, on the side where he wanted the tree to fall. Then he would chop at the opposite side, slightly higher than the first notch. Eventually, the tree should fall in the right direction, and the woodsman would shout, "Timber!" Felling trees was dangerous work, and the woodsman had to be careful of his own safety and that of the people with whom he was working.

After felling the tree, woodsmen would cut off the smaller branches and then use a barking iron to peel off the bark. Taking off the bark helped the wood dry and **season** faster. Usually wood was left to season for a year or more. When wood needed to be especially strong, as for a wagon wheel, it might be seasoned for four years.

Woodsmen working in the frontier were the foundation of the many woodworking trades.

At this stage, the wood was called timber. Often it would be cut into boards or planks, at which point it was called **lumber**. Pairs of sawyers would use long saws to split carefully marked logs into neat, regular boards. These were the right dimensions for many structures such as walls and floors.

Woodworkers were part of a vibrant colonial community of craftsmen and artisans, many of which were intertwined and dependent on each other.

With Which Wood Would a Woodworker Work?

When the colonists arrived in North America, they found a wide variety of trees. Some of these were familiar, and some were completely new. Different types of wood were ideally suited for certain uses.

Cedar wood was light and resistant to rot, so it was perfect for lightweight whaling boats, roof shingles, and buckets.

Tall, straight pine trees were perfect for ship masts. North American pines were so valuable that the British Navy marked the best ones for their own use, angering colonists.

Black oak resisted worm attacks, so it was used for the underside of ships. White oak and red oak were used for fence boards and barrel staves.

White ash was both flexible and strong, making it perfect for oars and tool handles (such as pitchforks).

Walnut and maple were prized for furniture making. Mahogany, imported from the Caribbean, was a high-status wood used for the finest furniture. Wealthy people also appreciated less common local woods such as apple, sassafras, and cherry.

Poplar wood could be cut very thin, and so was used to make lightweight boxes for storage and transportation of goods.

Locust wood was used to make "trunnels," the wooden pegs used as a substitute for iron nails.

FIVE

The Woodworker's Legacy

Although most wooden furniture and other wooden articles are now mass produced by machine, there is an enduring legacy of small craftsmen creating individual pieces by hand in much the same manner as America's earliest woodworkers. In places such as Colonial Williamsburg and other living heritage sites, craftsmen replicate the exact techniques used by colonial woodworkers. Many pieces of modern furniture are made in the same (or similar) designs as those that were popular in the seventeenth and eighteenth centuries. Variations such as the William and Mary, Queen Anne, and Chippendale styles are still popular today. Antiques in these designs can sell for large amounts of money.

Furniture from the colonial era can fetch high prices today. This Chippendale piece known as the Kenure Cabinet was recently auctioned for $5,324,767.

Colonial Toys

In the earliest days of the colonies, play and toys were frowned upon. There was work to be done, even by the youngest members

Hoops made of wood or the discarded metal tires from wagon wheels were popular children's toys.

of society. By the time a child was around seven or eight years old, he or she could shoulder some of the burdens of survival. Later, though, children had more time for playing, and by the Revolutionary War, the toy industry was becoming well established. Many of those toys were made from wood.

While few woodworkers probably specialized in toys, many would occasionally turn their talents to ornate rocking horses or other fun items for children. The Jacob's ladder was a favorite, consisting of wooden blocks held together with a ribbon, tumbling in a visual illusion. An elaborate model of Noah's Ark was also very popular, featuring Noah's family and tiny, paired animals made from wood. After the war, common wooden toys included spinning tops, popguns, wooden whistles, slingshots, and puzzles.

Another woodworking byproduct was a coveted toy: the metal tires used by wheelwrights to bind wooden wheels. These metal rings—when removed from broken wheels—were perfect for the favorite pastime of hoop rolling. Children would use a stick to roll the tire, seeing who would keep it upright the longest. They also performed tricks with these hoops and played other games.

William and Mary Style

The William and Mary style was popular until the 1720s. This style focuses on the vertical line rather than the horizontal line. That is, the furniture reaches upward instead of being low and heavy. It is known for its ornate design. Pieces were often lacquered or decorated with inlaid ivory. Comfort was starting to be important to colonists, and furniture started to be upholstered.

Queen Anne Style

In the later 1720s, furniture began to be less ornate and more restrained. This style was called Queen Anne, after the queen of Britain. Curved lines and classical proportions became popular. Furniture was even designed with the shape of a person's body in mind—chairs began to take on an S-curve to support the spine. A notable feature of the Queen Anne style was cabriole legs. These furniture legs were deeply curved to resemble goat legs, and were meant to suggest sprightly movement. Though Queen Anne designs were mostly more plain, a passion for the Far East made a process called "Japanning" popular. These pieces were decorated with colonial imitations of fantastical Asian scenes.

Chippendale Style

A woodworker named Thomas Chippendale literally wrote the book on this style, heavily influenced by the neoclassic French rococo. In *The Gentleman and Cabinetmaker's Directory* published in 1754, Chippendale favored this richly carved style. One of its signatures is the claw-and-ball foot, which makes the bottom of tables and dressers look as if they are supported by eagle or dragon talons.

Modern collectors value all of these styles, as well as more mundane wooden objects. Even common household objects of the period, such as wooden butter churns or bowls, are collected. The fact that some of the pieces have survived for more than three hundred years is testament to their fine craftsmanship. The colonial woodworkers set a high standard, and woodworkers today continue to follow in their footsteps.

Glossary

apprentice   A person bound to learn a trade from a master for a fixed period of years, usually for little or no pay.

colonist   A person who settles in a colony separate from their native country, such as the British settlers who came to America in the seventeenth and eighteenth centuries.

commissioned   Specially ordered or authorized.

gilded   Decorated with gold or gold leaf.

guild   An association of craftsmen practicing a particular trade, or of people having common interests or aims.

hardwoods   Wood from broadleaved trees such as oak (as opposed to wood from conifers or needled trees, such as pine).

Ice Age   A geologic period during which thick ice sheets covered vast areas of land.

joining   The woodworking specialty for connecting pieces of wood without metal fasteners.

journeyman   The stage after apprenticeship but before becoming a master; a journeyman could be paid for his work.

lathe   A machine used for rotating wood so that it can be shaped.

lumber   Timber that has been sawed into boards or planks.

master   A skilled practitioner of a craft, one who has passed through apprentice and journeyman stages, and created a masterpiece.

masterpiece   Something done or made with extraordinary skill or brilliance; a supreme achievement.

pitch   A thick, sticky substance derived from petroleum or tree resin that is used to create a waterproof seal.

season	Drying wood so it is ready for use.
shellac	A varnish derived from the excretions of the lac beetle.
softwoods	Woods of conifers, or needle-bearing trees such as pine or fir (as opposed to broad leaf trees such as oak).
speculation	Making a guess without firm evidence; in this case, creating a piece of furniture or other object without having a buyer in place.
timber	A tree or wood that has not been fully prepared for use.
turning	The woodworking specialty of shaping wood on a lathe.
utilitarian	Made to be practical or useful rather than strictly decorative.
varnish	A coating applied to wood to give it a hard shiny surface.
woodworker	A person who shapes wood into a decorative or useful form, such as a cabinetmaker, cooper, or carpenter.

Find Out More

BOOKS

Kalman, Bobbi, and Deanna Brady. *The Woodworkers*. Colonial People. New York: Crabtree Publishing Company, 2002.

Raum, Elizabeth. *The Dreadful, Smelly Colonies: The Disgusting Details About Life in Colonial America*. Minneapolis, MN. Capstone Press, 2011

Wilbur, Kiett C. *Home Building and Woodworking in Colonial America*. Old Saybrook, CT: The Globe Pequot Press, 1992.

WEBSITES

America's Story

www.americaslibrary.gov/jb/colonial/jb_colonial_subj.html

This site from the Library of Congress has articles that teach kids about many moments in American history. Explore its large section on Colonial America.

US History.org: Minutemen

www.pbs.org/wnet/colonialhouse/history

In the PBS series Colonial House, modern people tried to live exactly the way Colonial Americans did. Check out this interactive history website for information on the early colonial period.

MUSEUMS

Colonial Williamsburg

www.colonialwilliamsburg.com

This living history museum in Williamsburg, Virginia, recreates an entire colonial city. The 301-acre (121.8-hectare) site has many original historic buildings, and actor/docents who reenact colonial life. Explore stunning examples of American and British antiques and decorative art from the seventeenth, eighteenth, and nineteenth centuries.

The Metropolitan Museum of Art

www.metmuseum.org

The Metropolitan Museum of Art has an extensive collection of early American furniture. You may be surprised to discover that many of today's home furnishings are deeply tied to those of the past.

Index

Page numbers in **boldface** are illustrations. Entries in **boldface** are glossary terms.

About the Author

Laura L. Sullivan is the author of many fiction and nonfiction books for children, including the fantasy *Under the Green Hill* and the romance *Love by the Morning Star*. She has also co-written an upcoming romantic mystery set in the Golden Age of Hollywood, with famed director and producer Adam Shankman. She is the author of many books for Cavendish Square, including six titles in the Colonial People series.